Curious Design

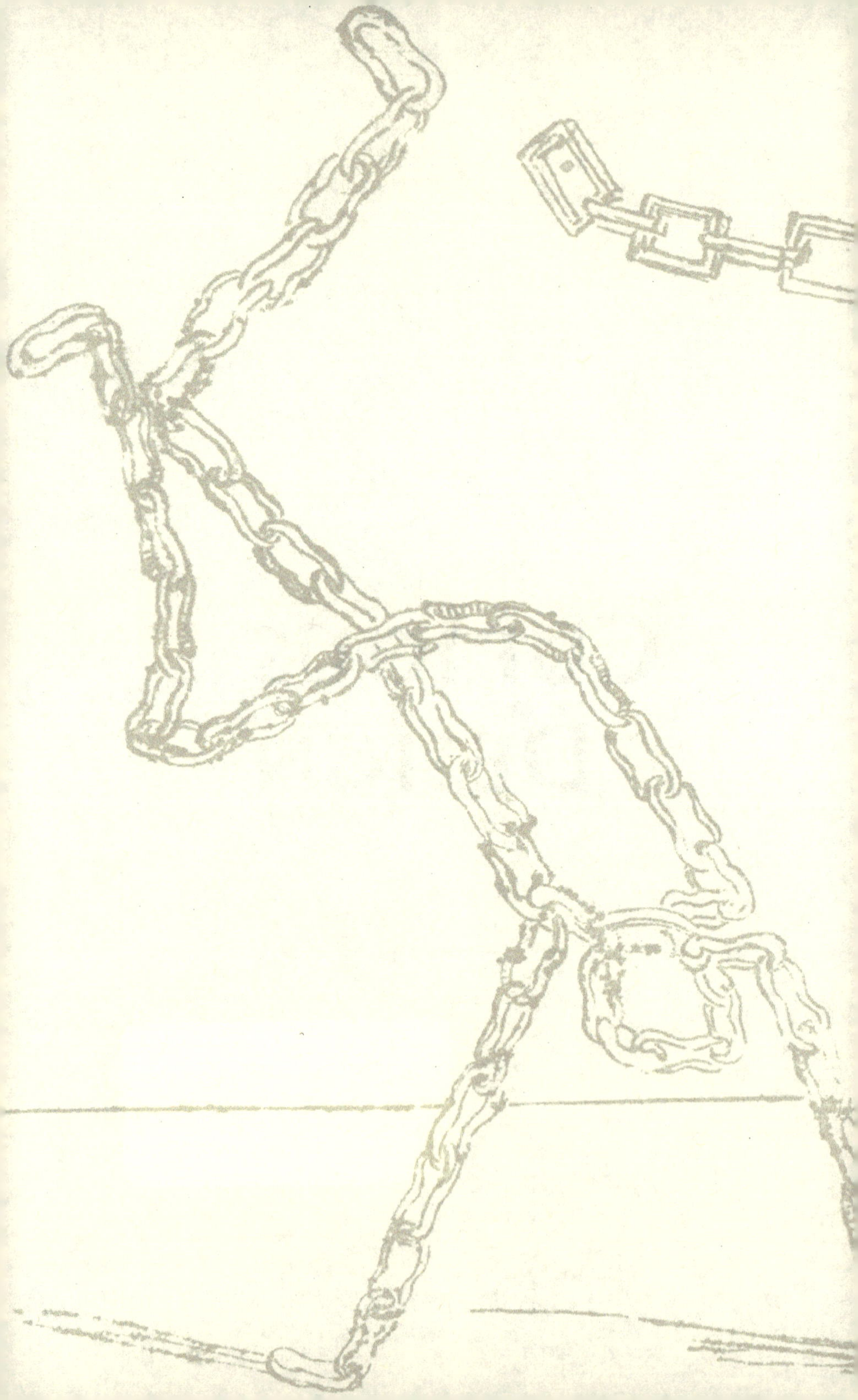

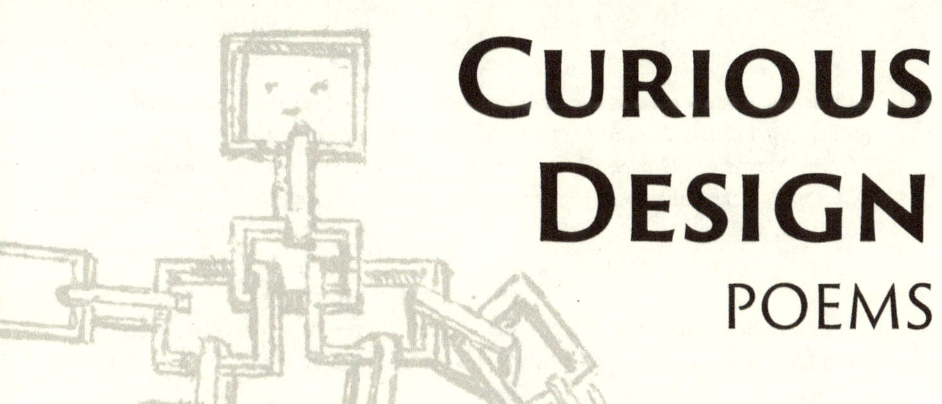

Curious Design

Poems

Bonnie Stanard

Belle Isle Books
www.belleislebooks.com

These poems are excerpts from poems that have been previously published in the following journals: *Muddy River Review*; *Scarlet Leaf Review*; *Hiram Poetry Review*; *Moon Magazine*; *Gravel*; *Slant*; *White Ash Literary Magazine*; *Constellations*; *Chiron Review*; *Lalitamba*; *Slipstream*; *The Griffin*; *Eclipse*; *RE:AL*; and *The South Carolina Review*.

Art

Bracelli, Giovanni Battista, active 1624-1649. Bizzarie: Propos sur Bracelli/par Tristan Tzara. L'aventure d'un livre et notes bibliographiques, par Alain Brieux, éditeur. Paris : 1963.
2 v. : ill. ; 19 x 25 cm.
NE662.B66 B7

Giovanni Battista Bracelli was an Italian engraver and painter working in Florence, Italy, in the 17th Century. The artwork here is taken from his book of prints titled *Bizzarie di Varie Figure* (Oddities of various figures). In forty-seven plates he portrayed interacting human figures, their forms made of cubes, rings, and squares, as well as rackets and screws. A digital copy of the original manuscript can be found at the Library of Congress.

ISBN: 978-1-958754-07-8
Library of Congress Control Number: 2022919762

Printed in the United States of America

Published by
Belle Isle Books (an imprint of Brandylane Publishers, Inc.)
5 S. 1st Street
Richmond, Virginia 23219

BELLE ISLE BOOKS
www.belleislebooks.com

belleislebooks.com | brandylanepublishers.com

for Doug

Also by Bonnie Stanard

Poetry

Time Carries All Things Away

Prose

Béjart's Caravan
Dust On the Bible
What Missing Means
Kedzie, St. Helena Island Slave
Master of Westfall Plantation
Sonny, Cold Slave Cradle
Westfall, Slave to King Cotton
Cat's Fur
Lizard Brew
Tenth Full Moon

Table of Contents

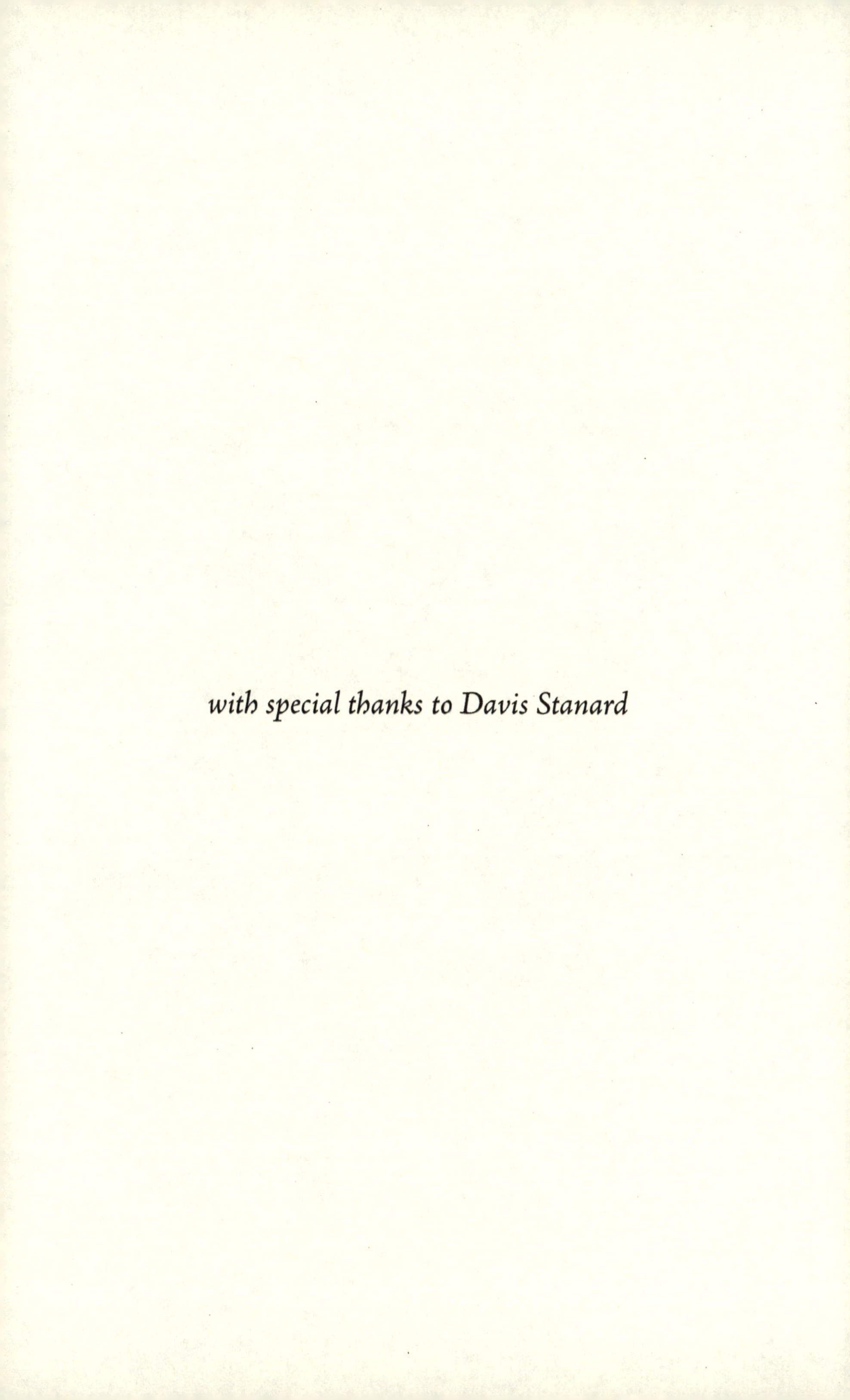

with special thanks to Davis Stanard

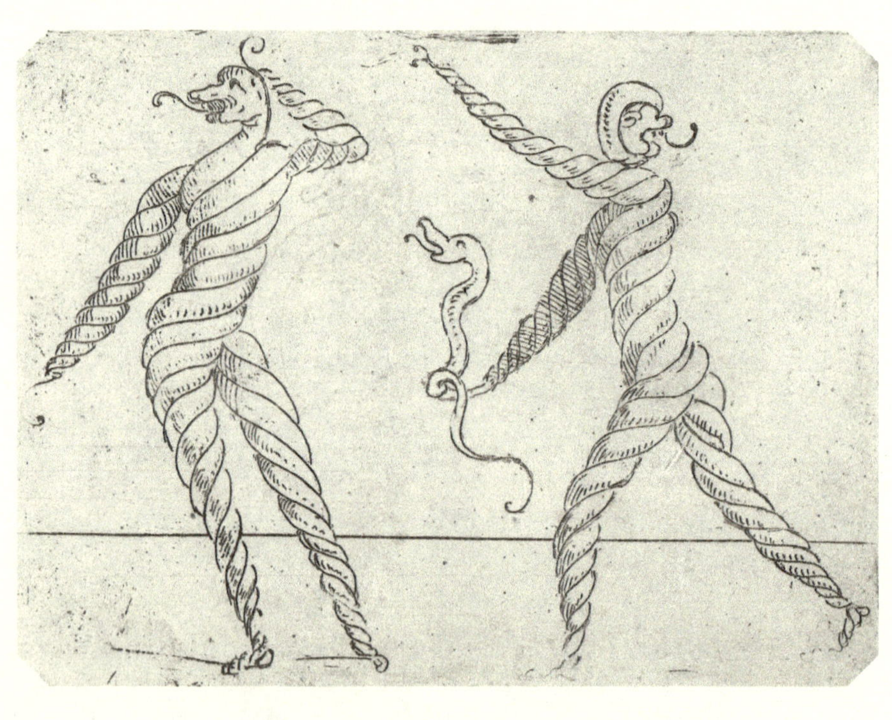

Rain

Some people speak of soft rain
or a gentle shower. And yes,
there was a time when a tin roof told me
rain's gentle story and I believed it.
But today things are different.

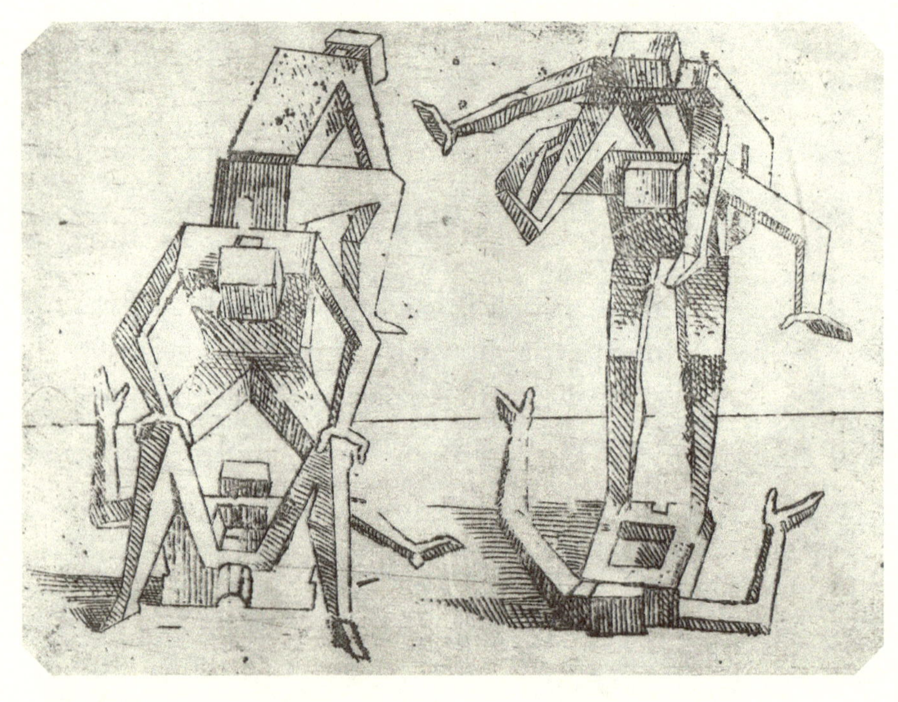

SURVIVAL

The rough and tumble of gangland relatives
taught me to run and hide when I could
and when I couldn't, to tell lies and fight dirty.

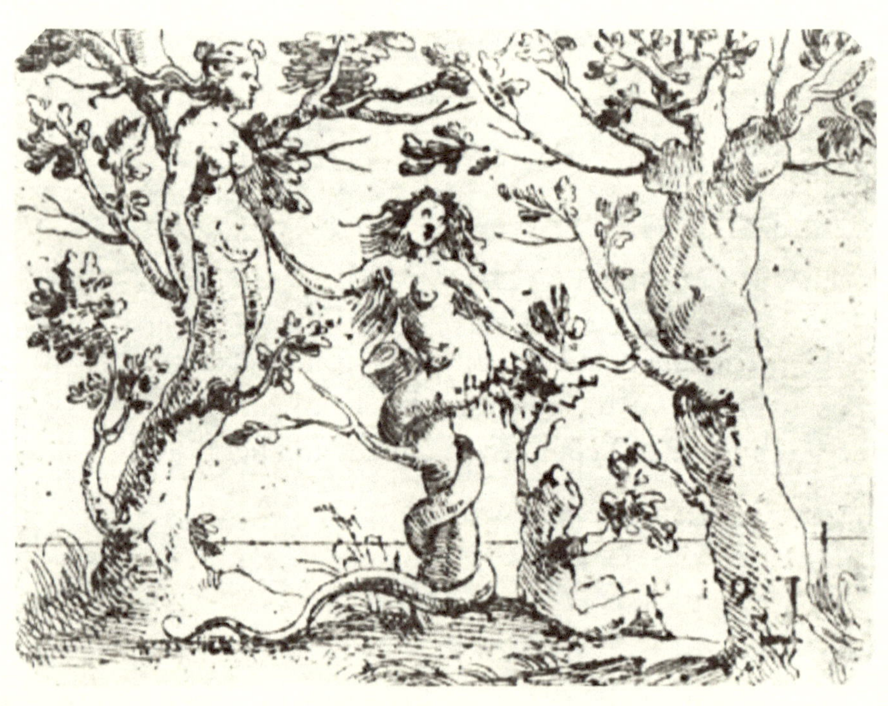

ROOTS

Once I felt at one with the sky.
I thought I had inborn clouds,
whether restless or calm.
I had in my blood rain and sunshine.

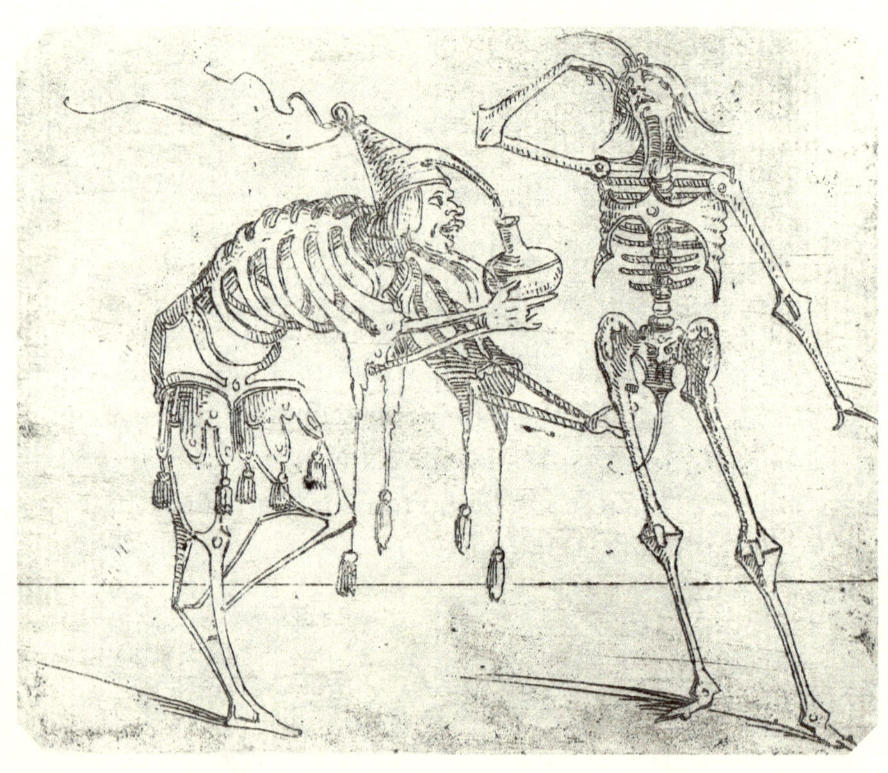

Lesson

I was afraid to complain
because this one life
was all I was going to get.
That much I understood.

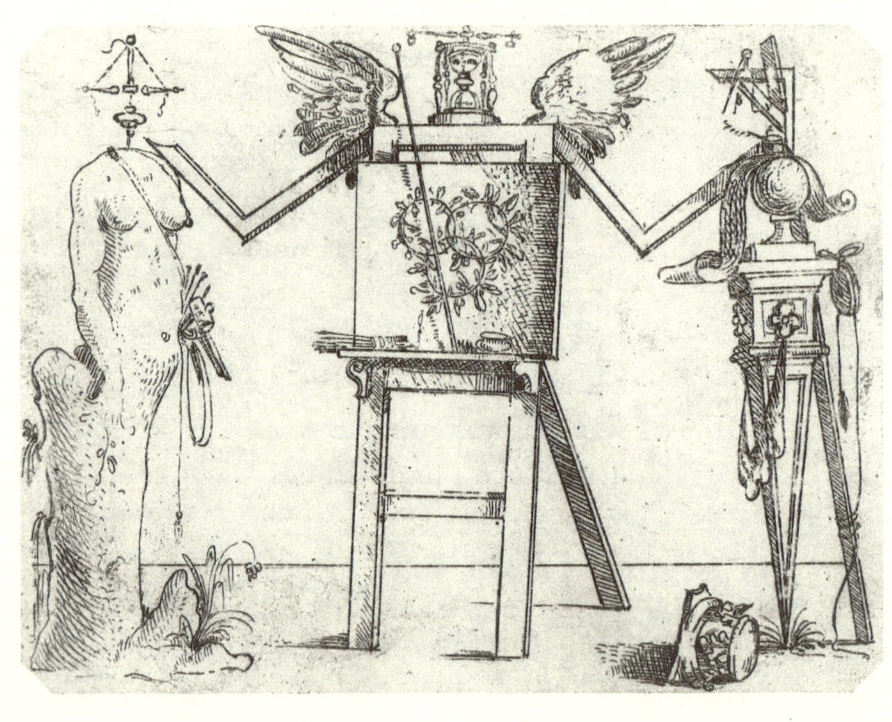

Ambition

Fixing things up
is what I try to do
even if it means giving up
habitation in trees
and treks to junkyards.

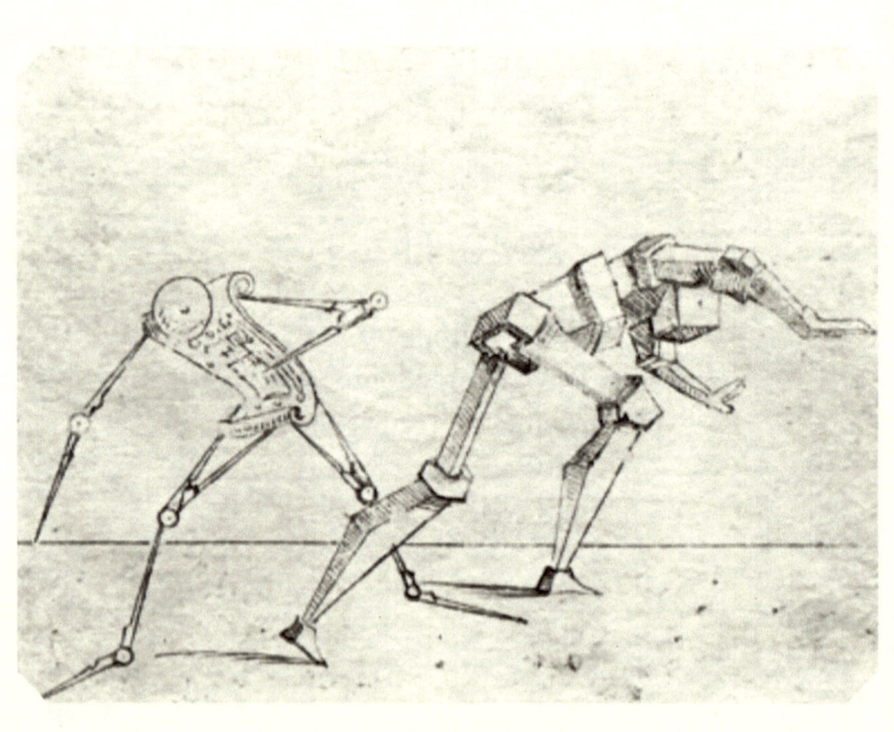

Blurry

Sometimes commercials get in your eyes
and shed doubt about whatever happens
and how much it costs.

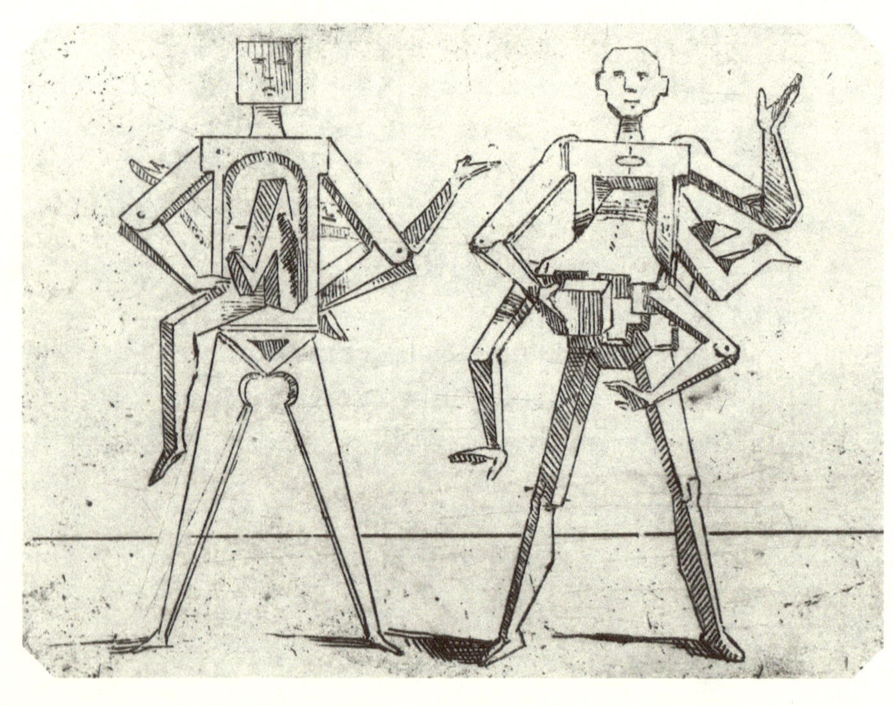

Residue

Some people say we eat fallout
if clouds travel
from a nearby reactor
and rain on our grain.

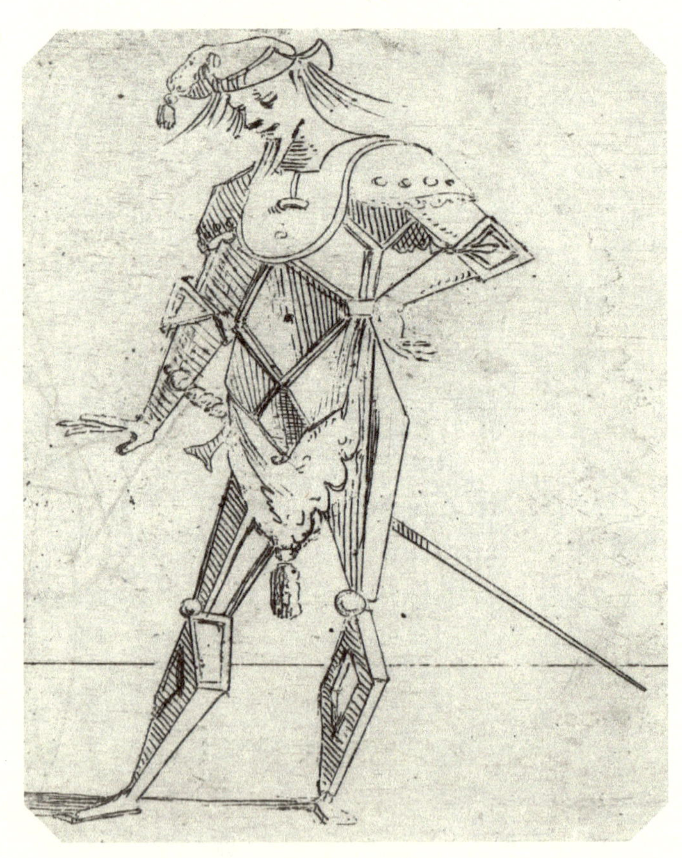

UMBRELLA

Who wants to walk in the rain
if it smells like a paper mill
and feels like crinoline?

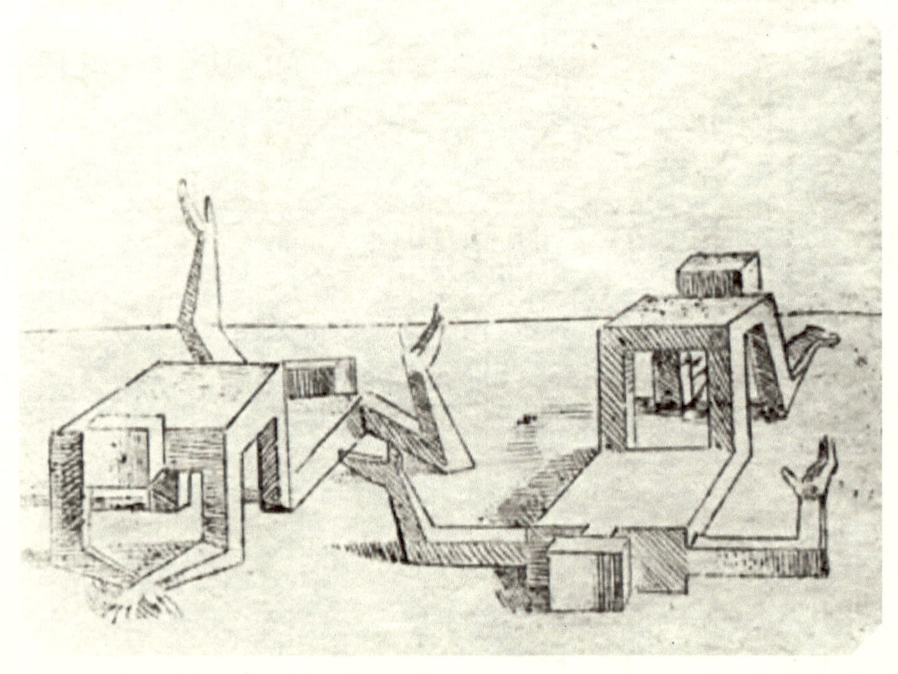

Login

I don't meet strangers
much less friends,
and my social life
comes down to my computer
and conversations with apps.

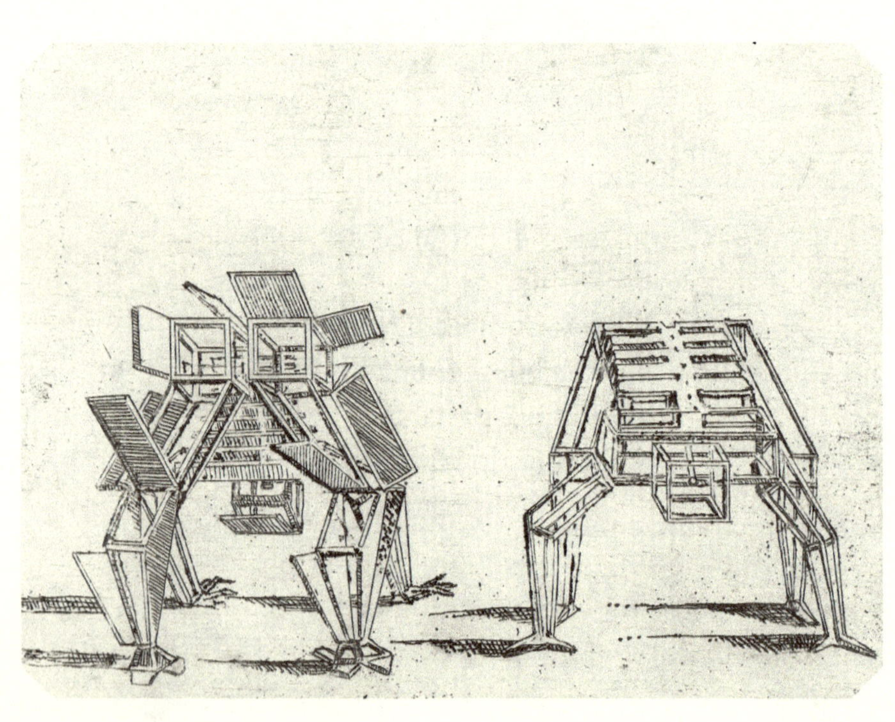

SURFING

My browser interfaces my eyeballs
and searches for a site
capable of suspending the end of time.

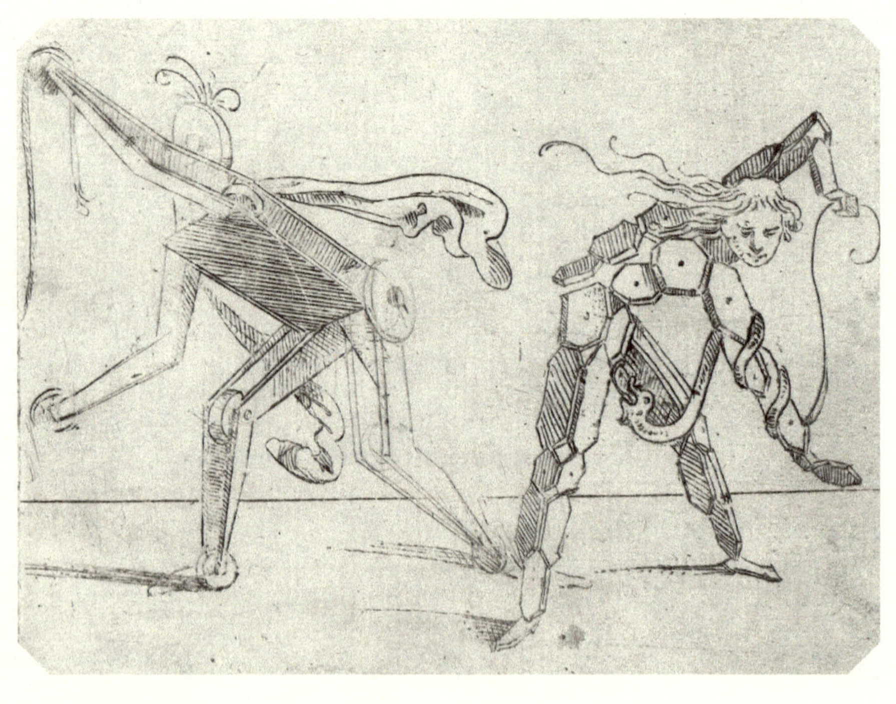

ORBIT

It makes me anxious to see
epiphanies fly by in gigabytes,
especially when it's late
and I can't see the clouds
outside my window.

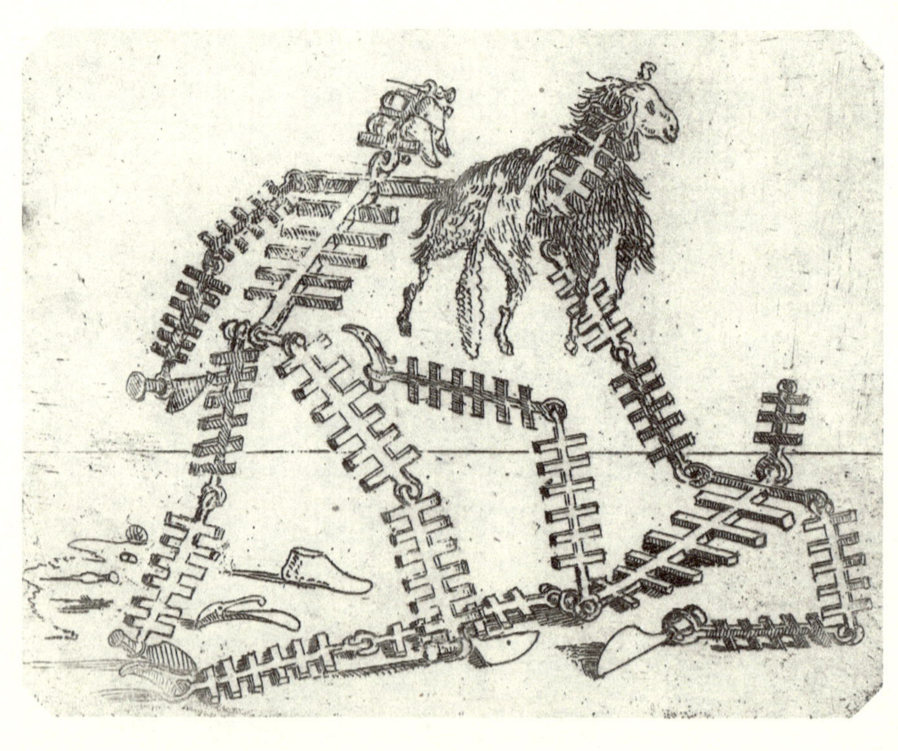

Hardwired

As cyberspace replaces time,
some scientists suggest
that the heartbeat behind electric current
is experiencing irregular voltage.

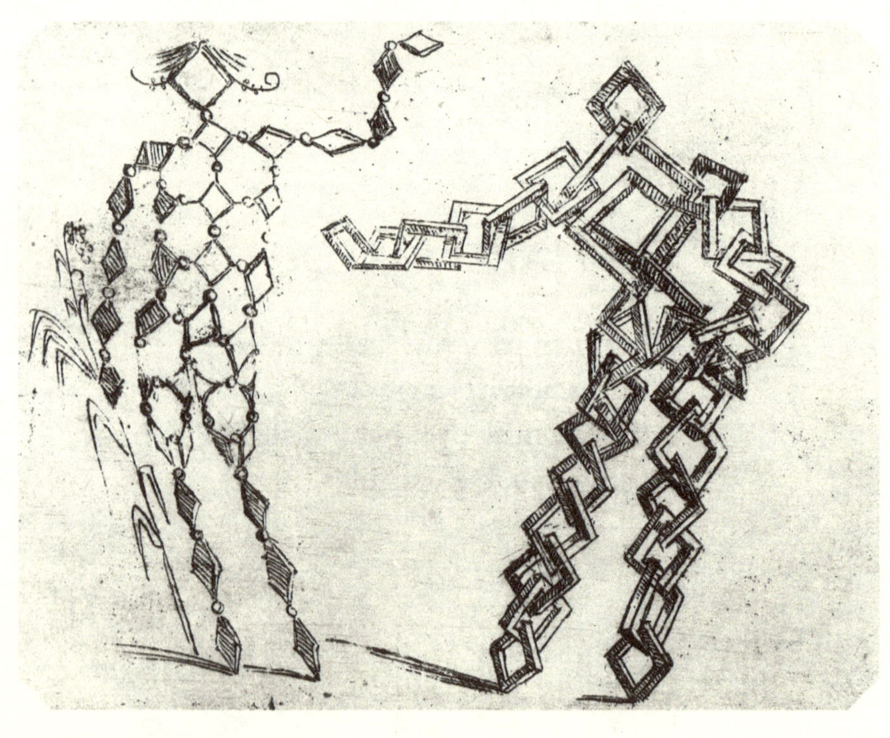

SPAM

Regardless of the links I've traveled
and the addresses I've visited,
countless domains remain,
so many locations
and so many people
who can live without me.

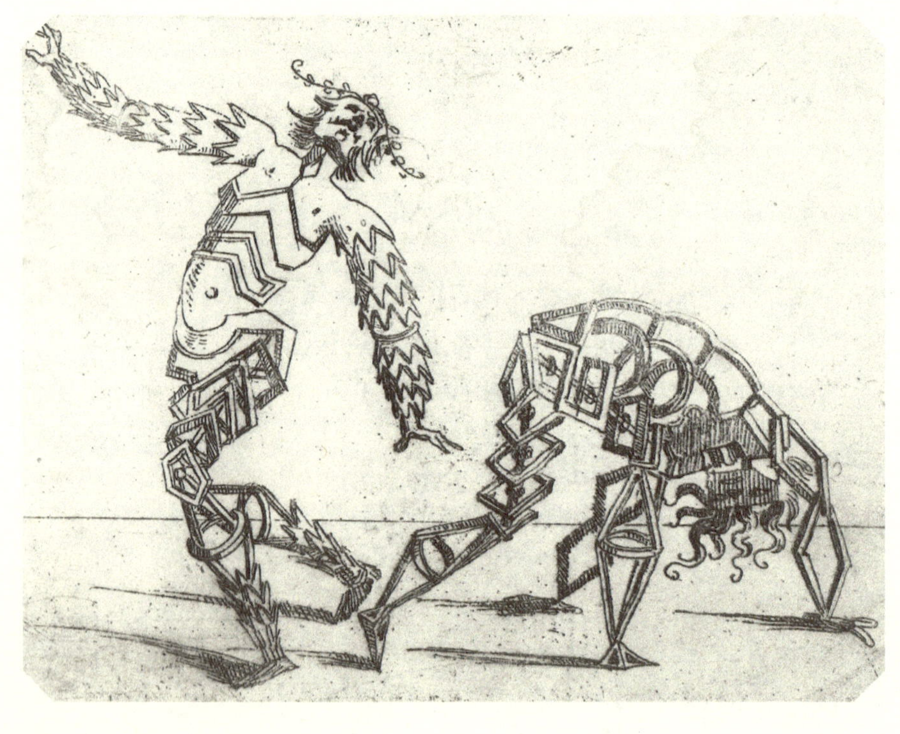

Tonic

Perhaps too much wine
is in my blood
or a bad dream
is in my head,
but the walls chase me
in cycles defying viewpoint.

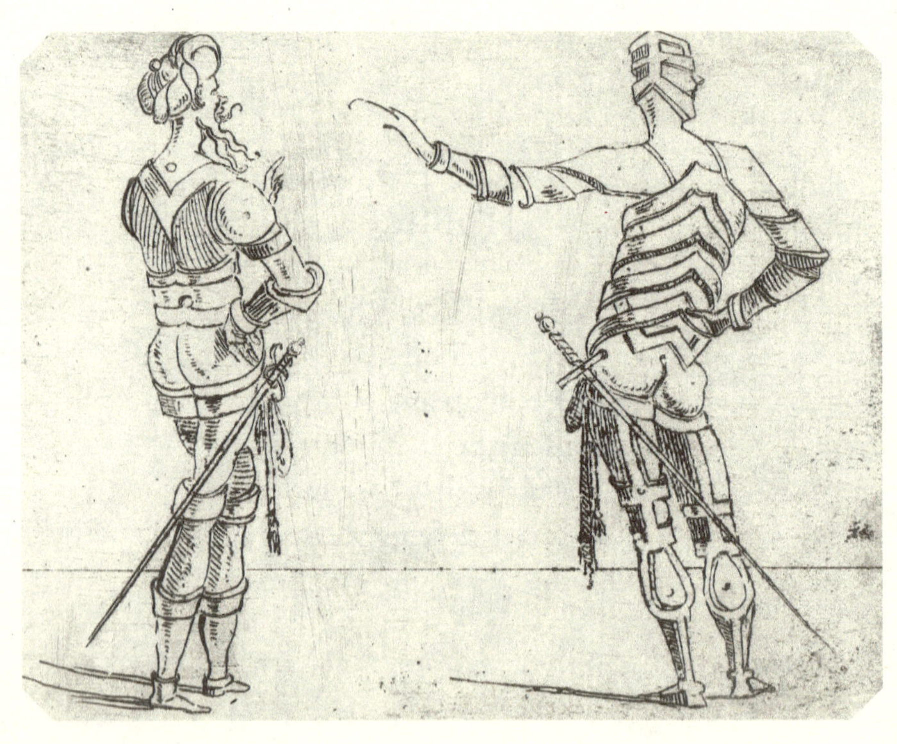

Hotline

My amorous affairs,
bordering on love of memory
and its long shadow,
are overdue for a makeover.

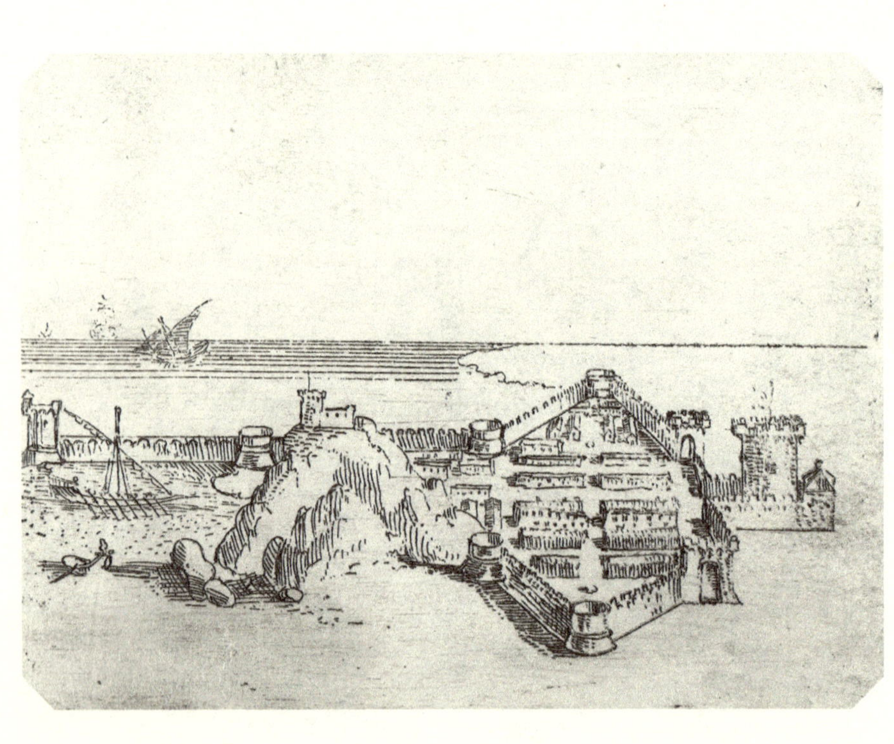

POLARITY

With pale skin and freckles
I usually settle for a summer singe,
but just down the street is a salon
advertising everlasting suntans.

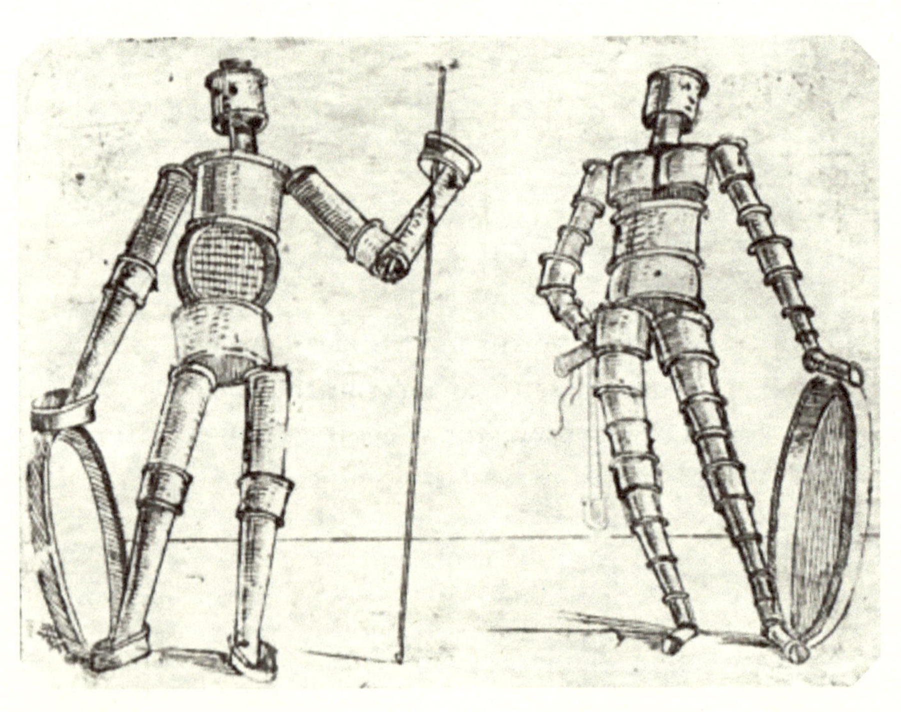

SYMBOLISM

In my closet are original,
before-the-fact, retro fashions
that I don't wear
in case a mirror ages me with my clothes.

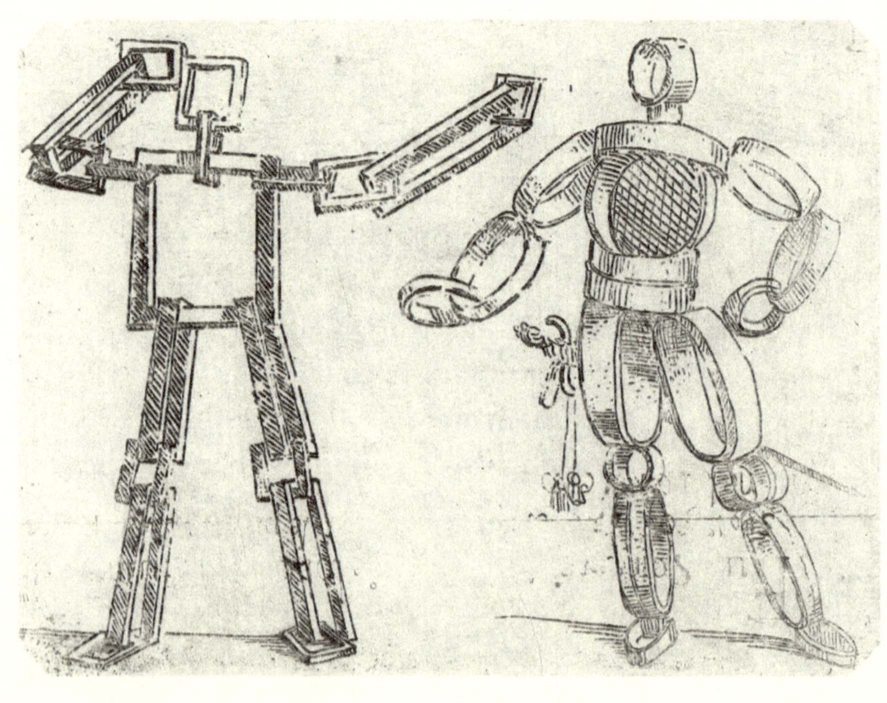

Obsession

I look at myself often to detect early signs
of antecedents in the eyes.

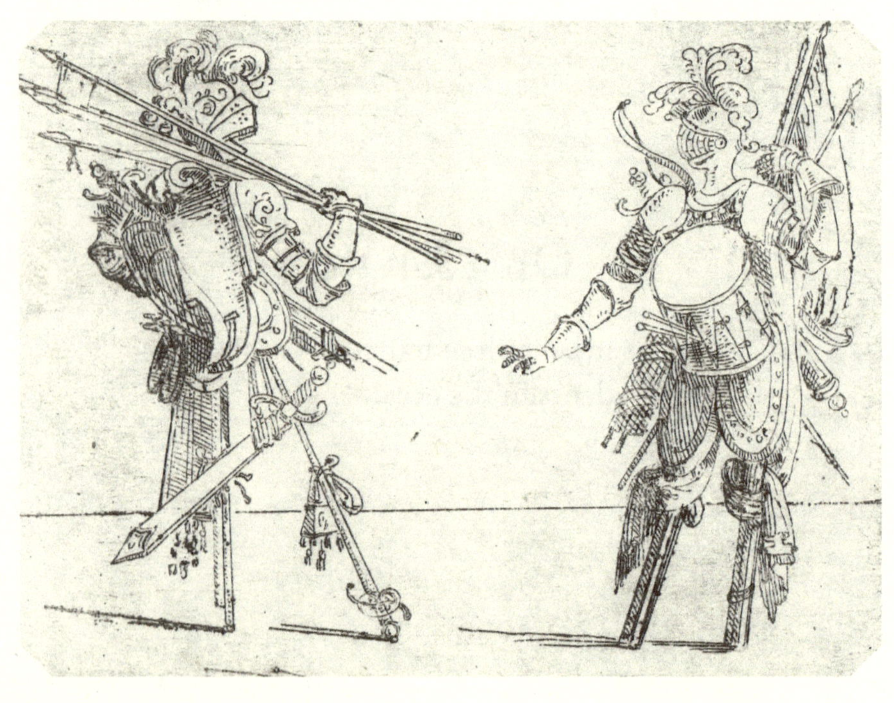

Indulgence

My mall rat karma goes on a fashion bender.
I haul home bags of fantasy, latex pants,
and an unlimited supply of sass in silk.

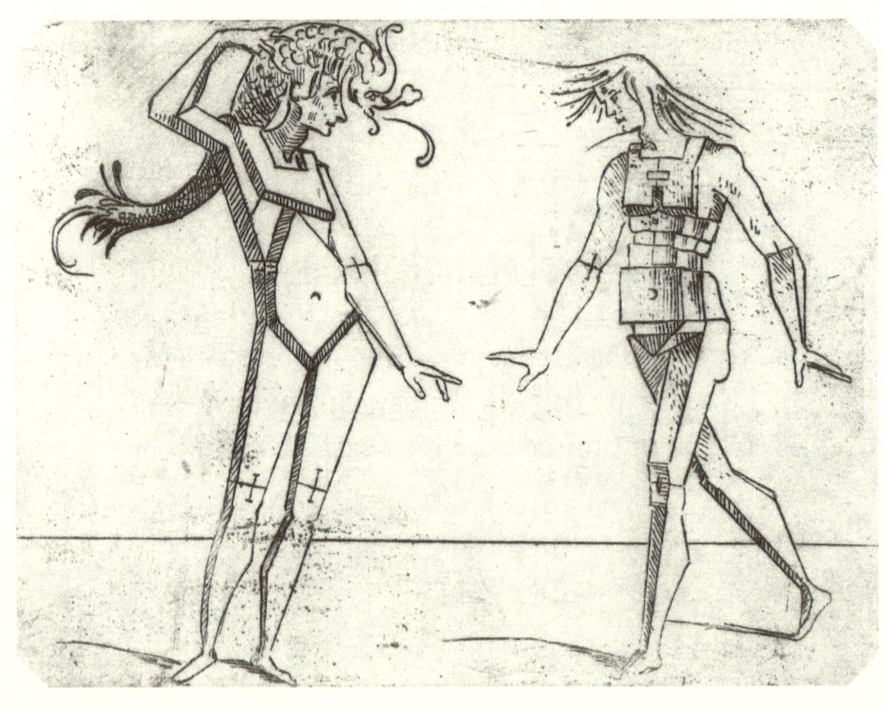

Ritual

Everything safe is for suckers.
I've come a long way. I can kickass.
I'm not some stupid little anxiety
in a black dress. Look closely.
The deepest dirt conditions me.

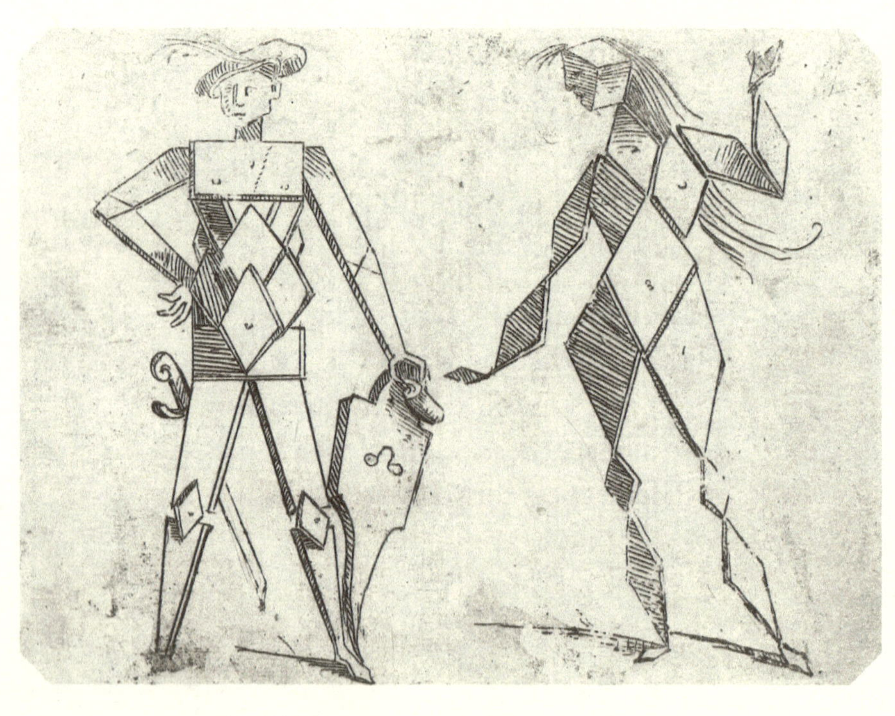

TECHNIQUE

When I feel a dread coming on
I might drink scotch and water
or pick up cocktail characters
and pummel my bed into a ratty cave.

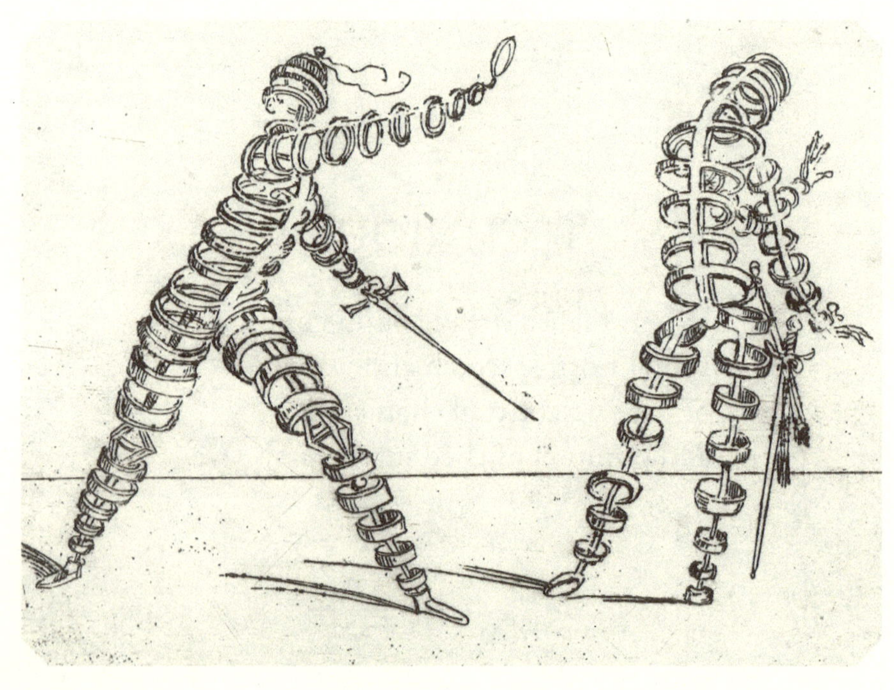

Wordy Sips at the Bar

Thursday night is sweet and intense.
With rivalry ready to commit revelry,
a silver edge on every word,
even sub-zero philosophy blows smoke
and rebounds in flight.

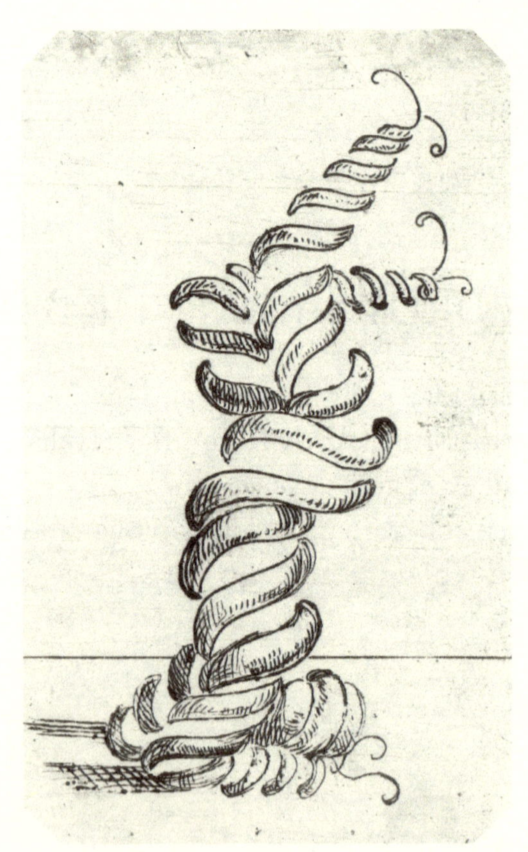

VOLTAGE

Pleasure's on the phone
and I have putty fingers
and a memory of soaring,
was it last Friday?

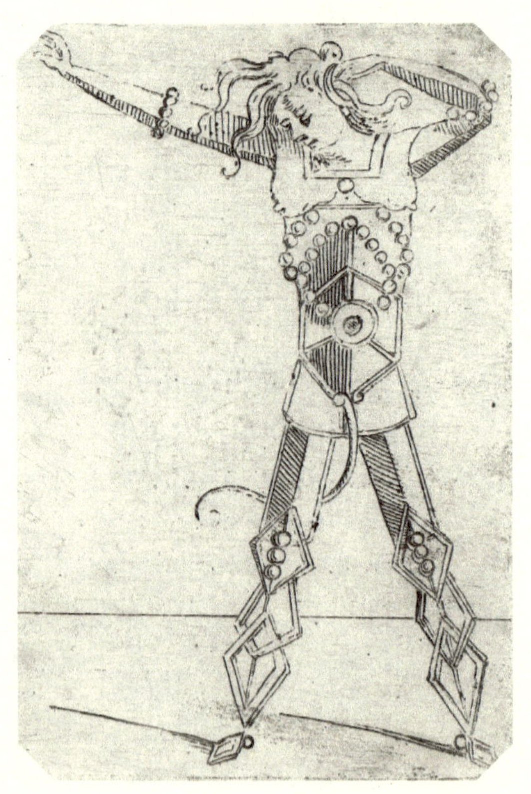

FIREDAMP

I'm a wide-lipped woman
slipping in and out of a person
in the manner of music
entering and in pleasure
so hammering
my skin thrums
with unnatural warmth.

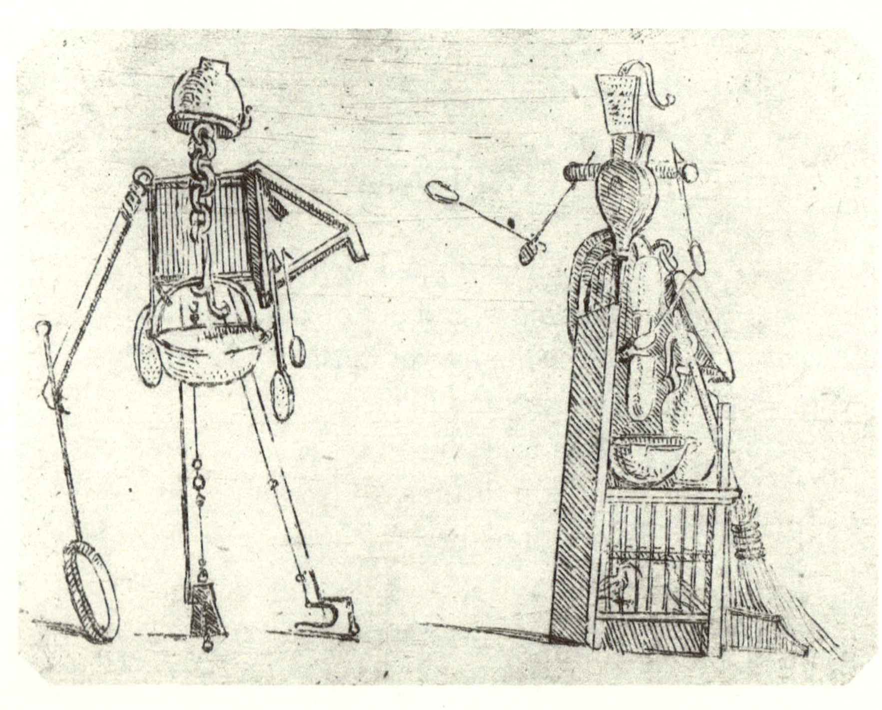

Inert

Today the time's not right
or the wind's blowing
from the north
or maybe it's the bad vibes
in my bones.
Anyway, I can't do it.

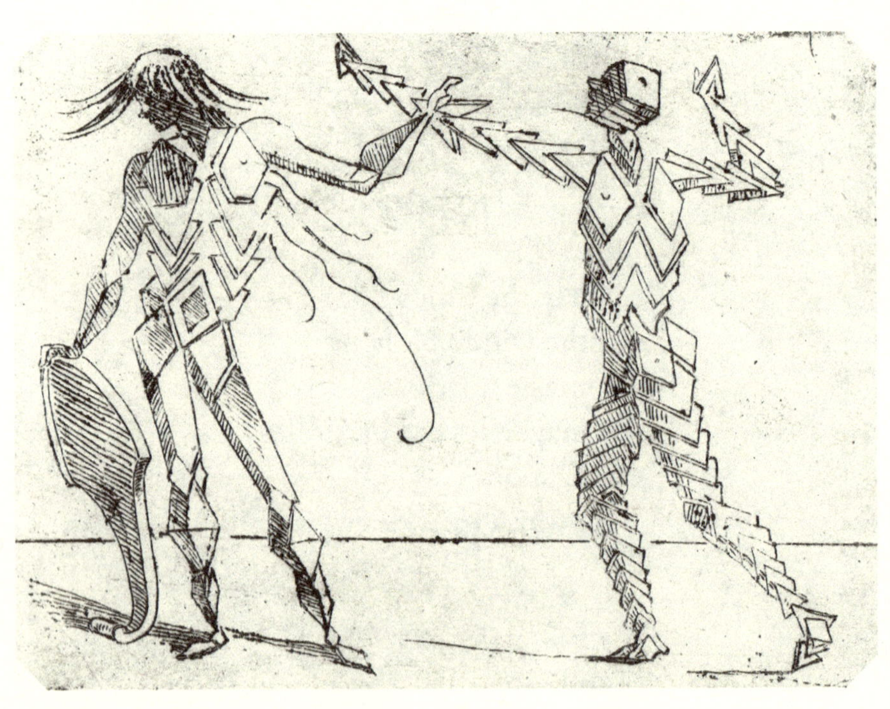

Neutral

Maybe the ground isn't real.
Birds flying by seem to be saying
"Ready to go,"
"Take one step,"
"Anytime now,"
but since I'm already happy,
I see no need to make any changes,
and the wind is nice too.

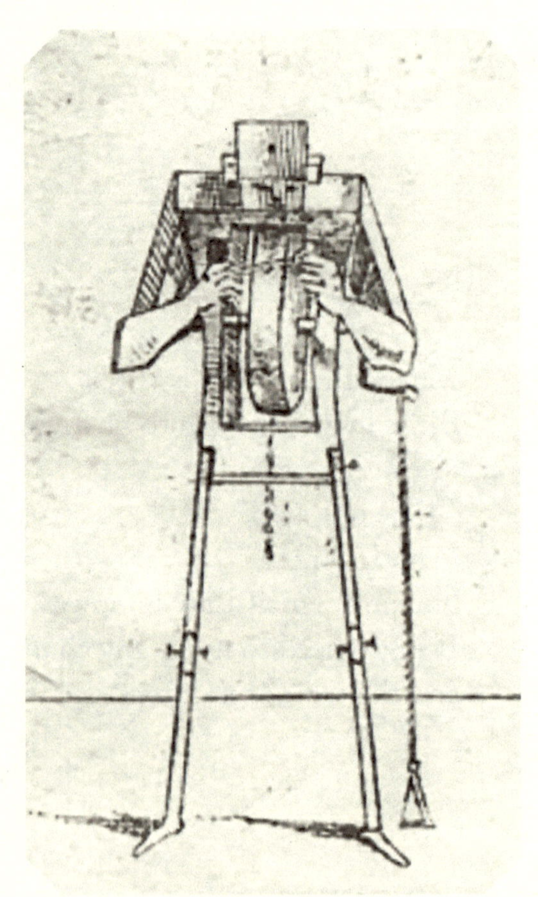

Cool Coat

There are nightmares in my clothes
too close to have names.
I've expected love before
though my tongue doesn't show it.
"I do," I can't, even if he's cute.

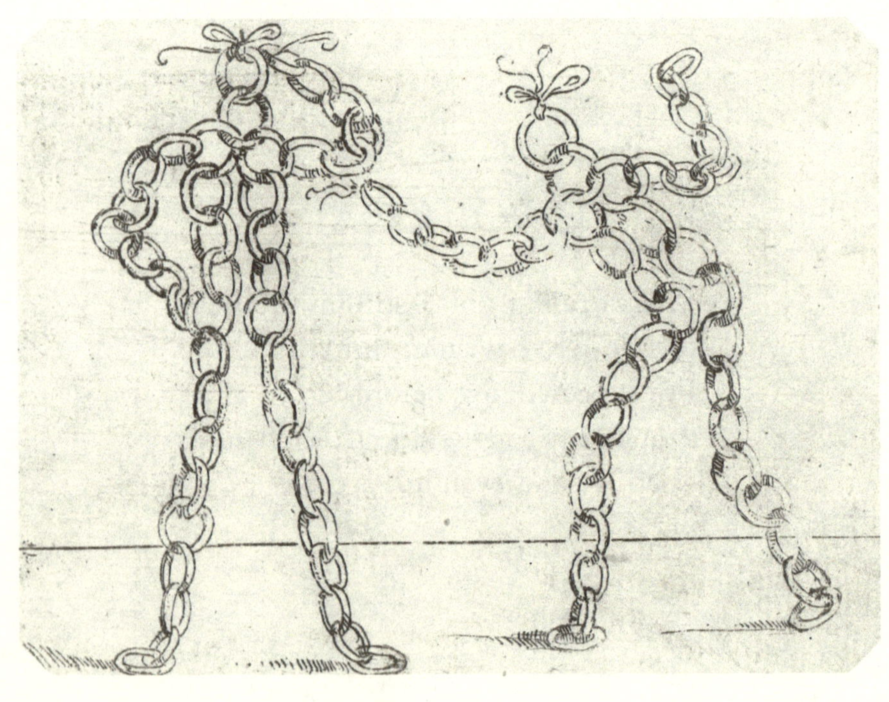

Blister

Your comfortable distance
isn't easy to estimate.
What do you mean
by mutually acceptable space?

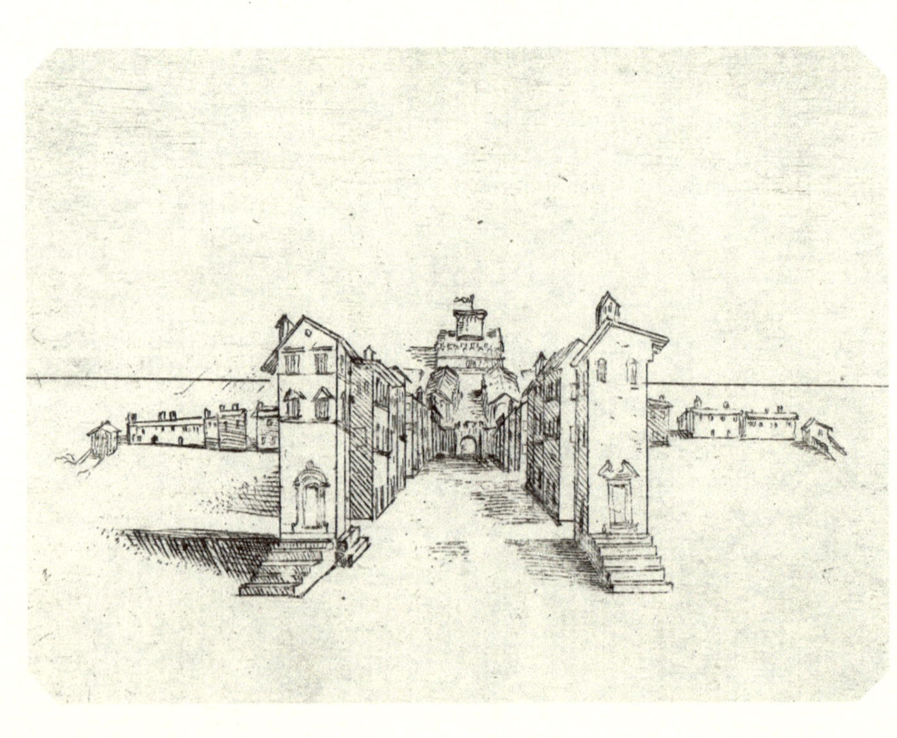

Coronary

A morning broke without warning
and I woke up alone,
for he was in love but without me.

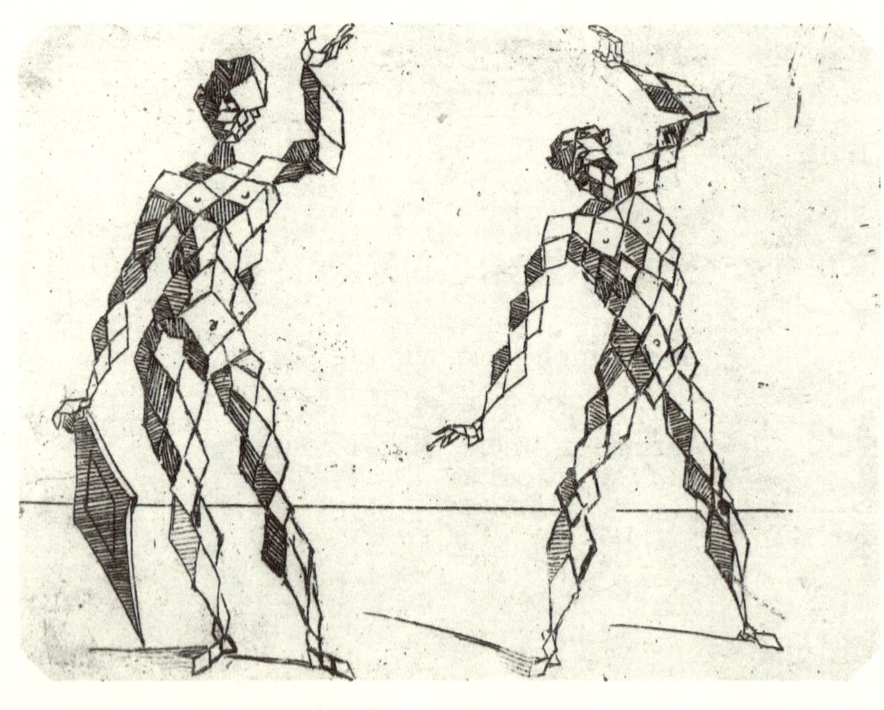

Tracer

Perhaps it was because
he enjoyed the symphony
and I pretended to.

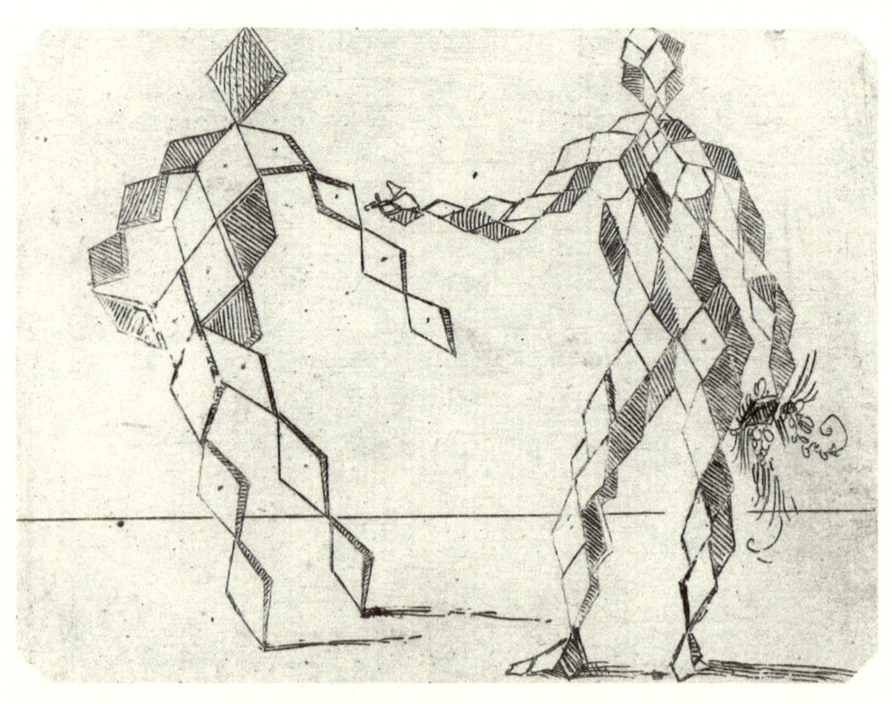

FLUX

My already skin is beginning the weekend back in the bag. I'm bad another Saturday.

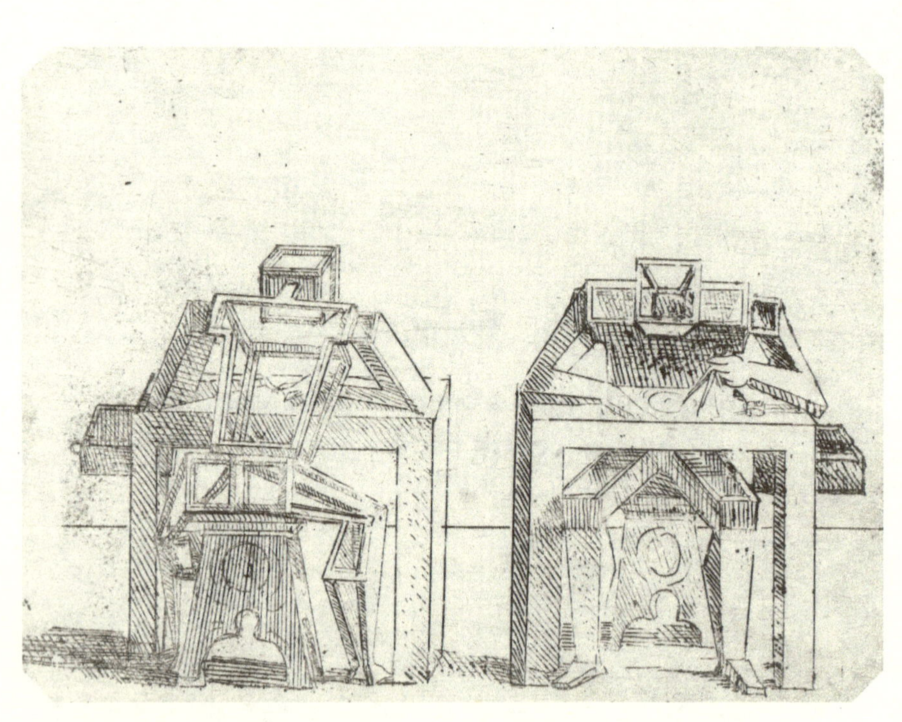

FLIGHT

Some people retreat to melodrama
mostly in front of a television,
but in worst case scenarios
they slip into a coma called routine.

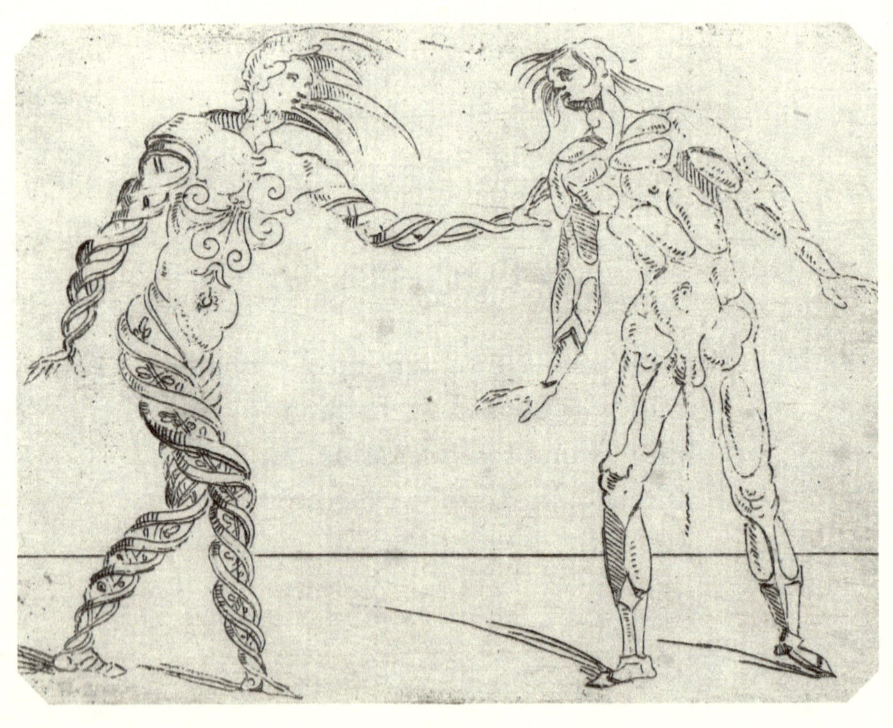

NEBULA

I always listen
to what the meteorologist has to say
even if I have doubts about the nature
of motion in the atmosphere.

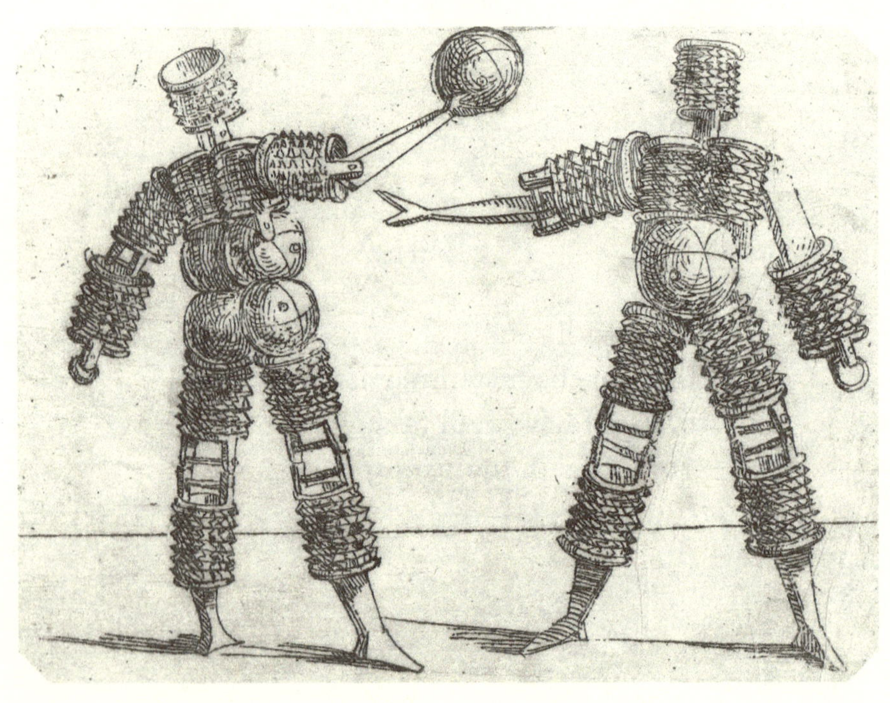

Plight

I realize I am dwindling
my immortality account
with faith in fleshly desires,
investments in false profits.

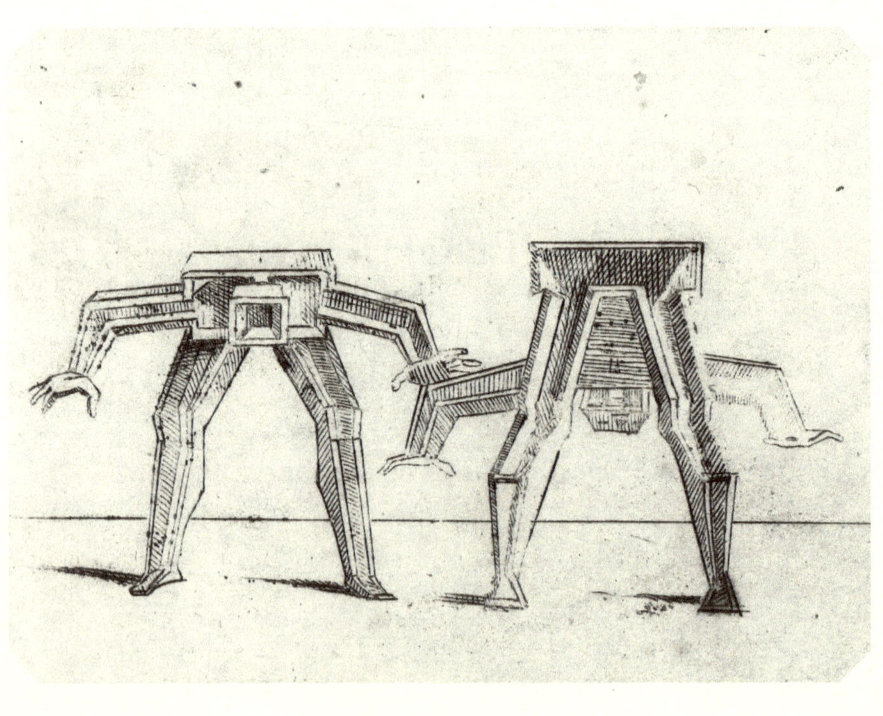

Outflow

Subject to pallor, ulcers,
and above all, high blood pressure,
I see my minutes and hours leak
through cracks in the kitchen floor.

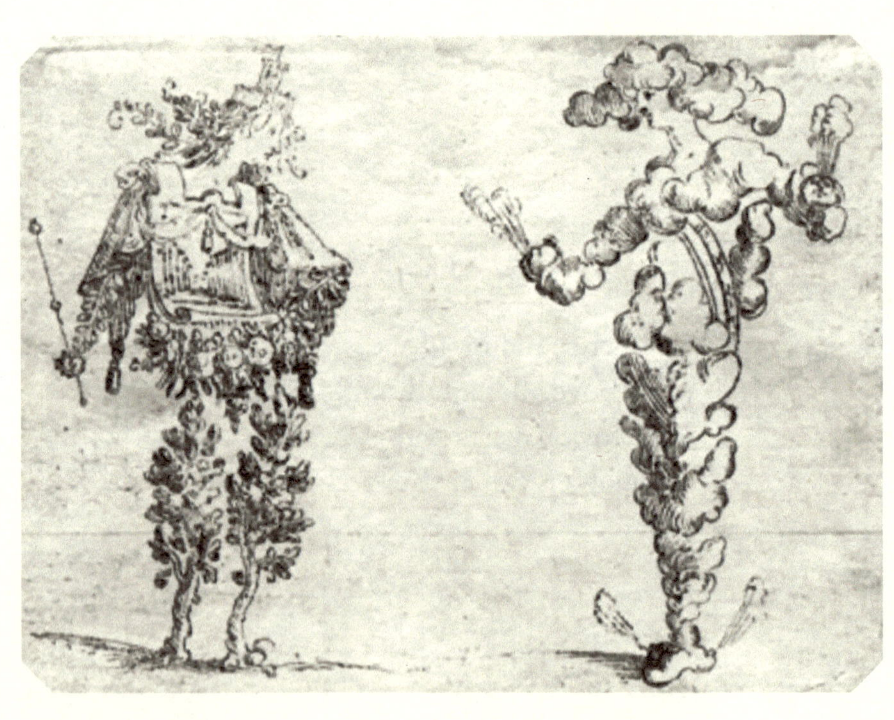

SUBSTRATUM

It doesn't seem appropriate
to think of birth as defeat
but uninvited stones
are in the church yard.

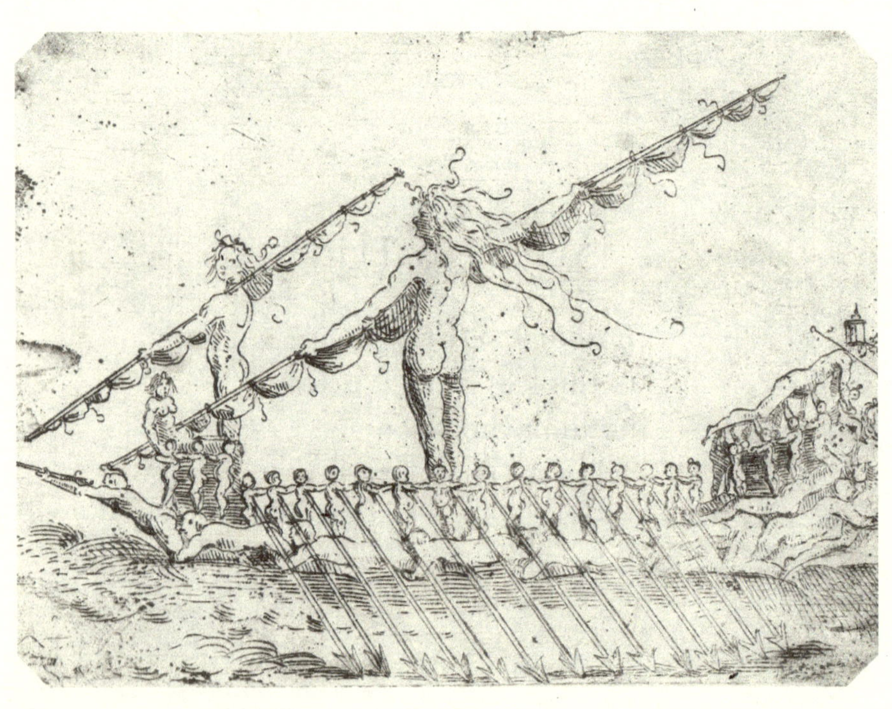

Opacity

With the passage of the present
I am persuaded
by all that's green and mumbles
that nobody knows why we say goodbye.

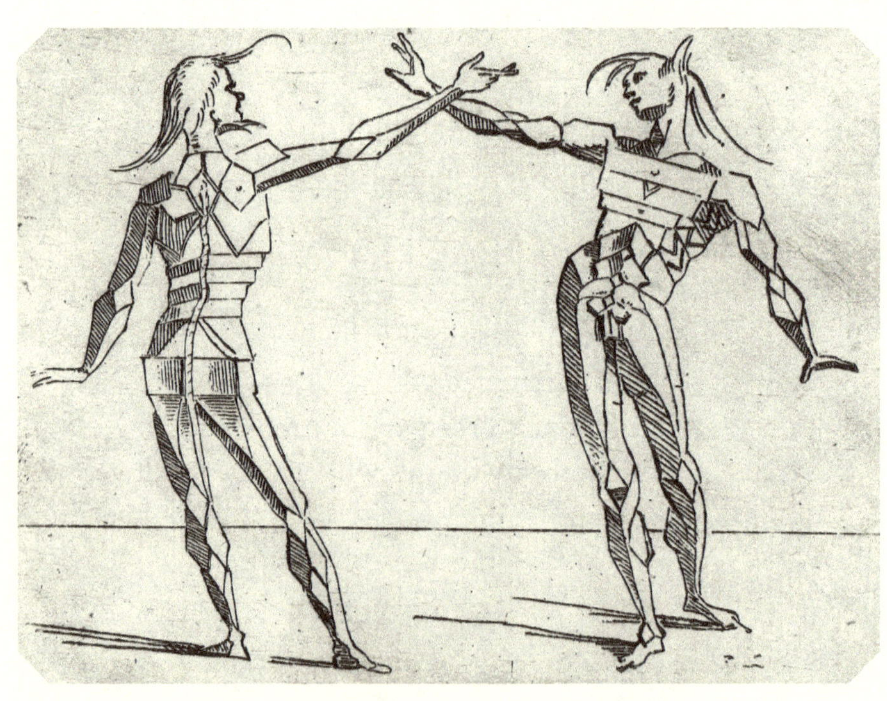

Allotment

Did my mother inherit
from untold mothers
the obsession to see
the beginning,
the black eye
of our universe?

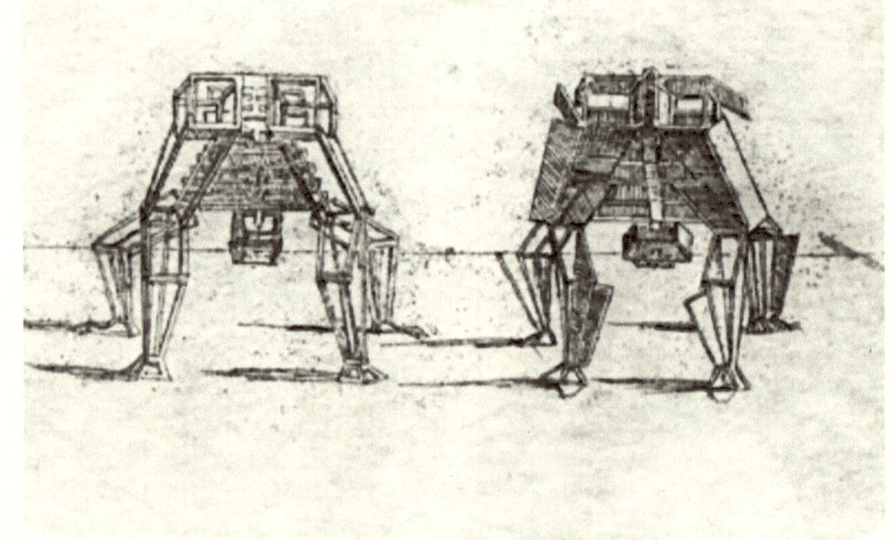

Pivot

Living comes with one ear to the ground,
and even those without religion realize
heartbeats are God's timers.

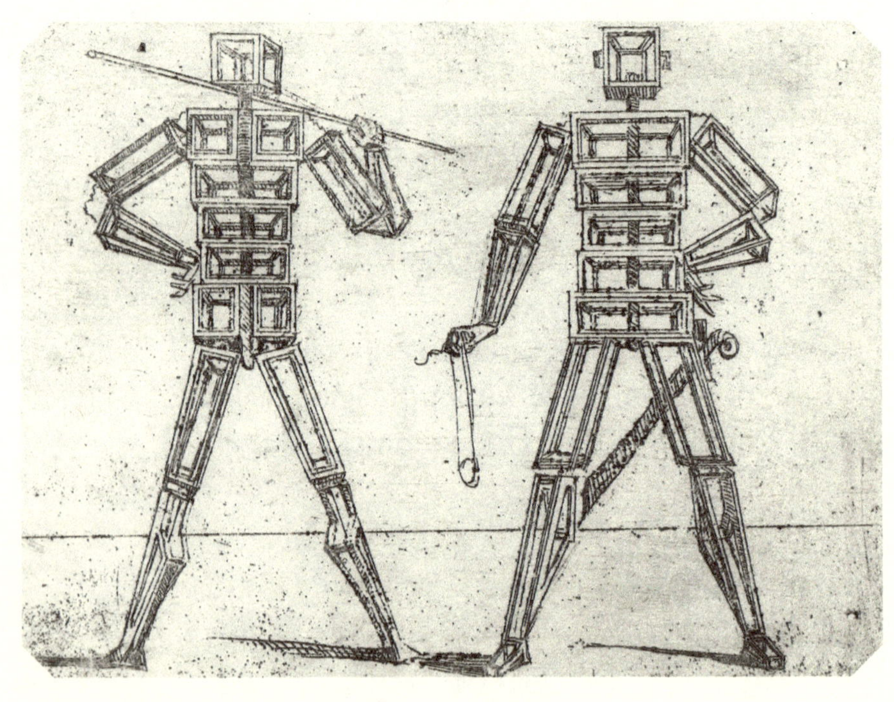

CREDO

I trust in unseen things
as if reliability is innate.
I choose a religion
with the best reality show.

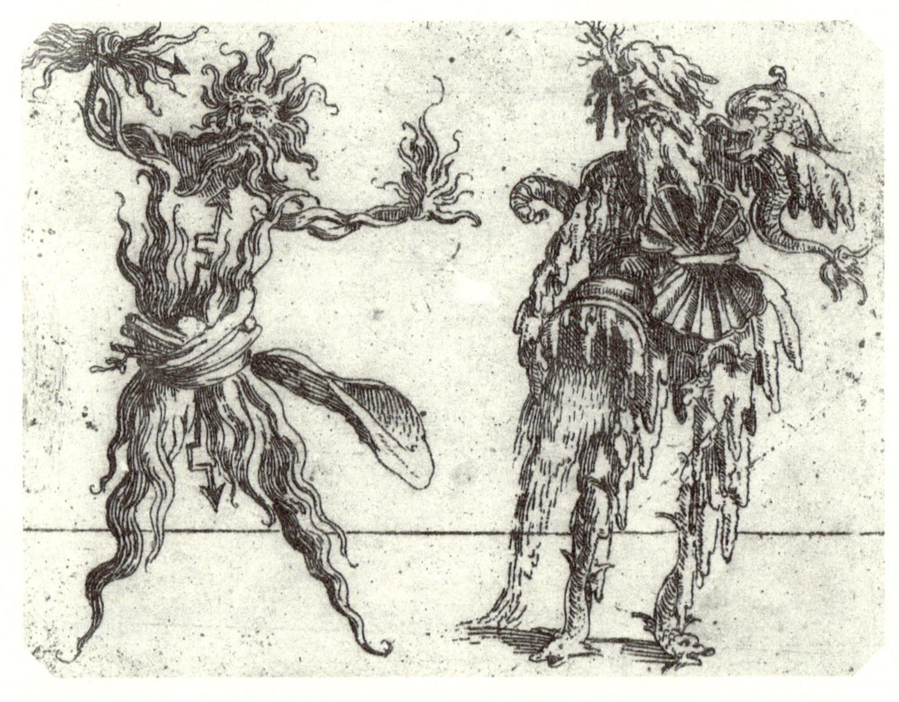

INSECTICIDE

I heard it from my many friends
that if you repeat what God says,
nightmares won't grow in your backyard.

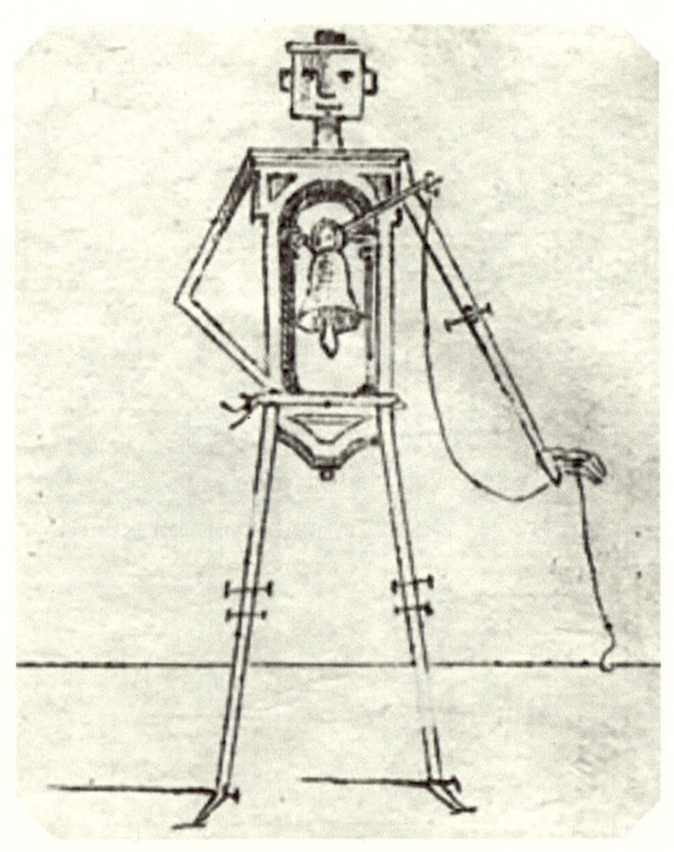

Billboard

There's an oak tree in front of me
whose worship I know.
Hallelujah is written in leaf letters
against the sky.

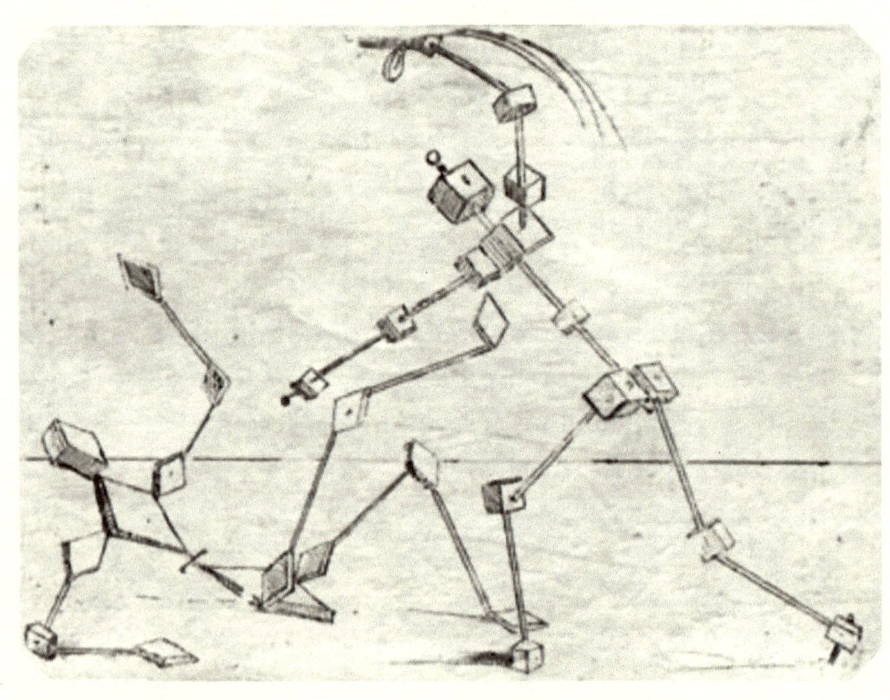

PREFIX

I pray for insights to save me
from the utter folly
of originating sin, something
I think I'm good at.

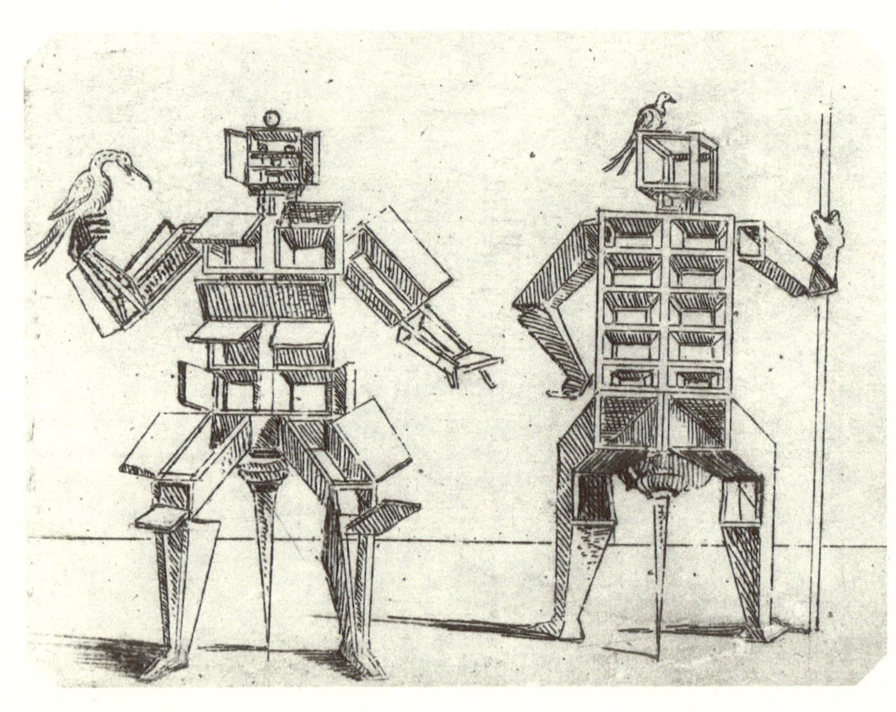

IMPOTENT

In my dreams
I am with my father when his heart stops,
when he recognizes his end
with "Oh shit!"

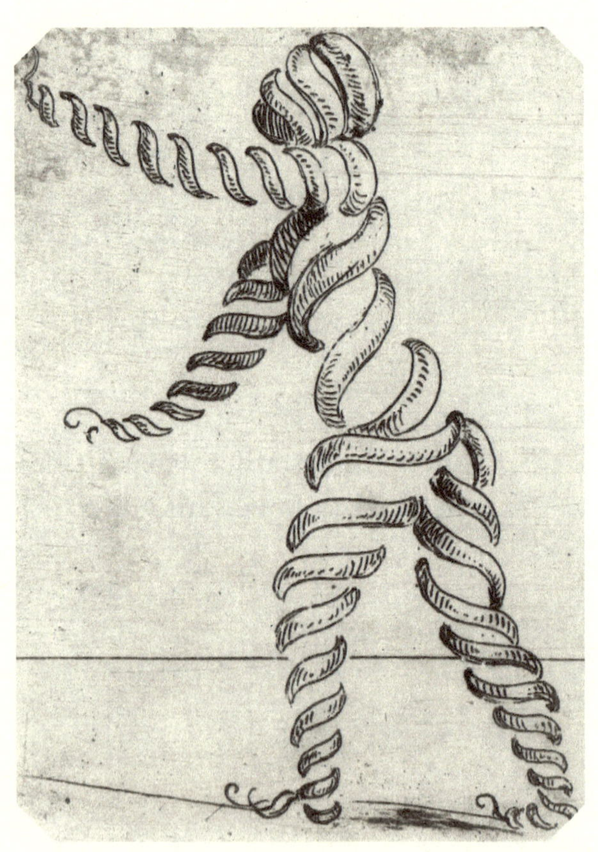

Borders

My father speaks in stars
that tell horizons.
I listen for his voice,
but stars don't make
audible sounds.

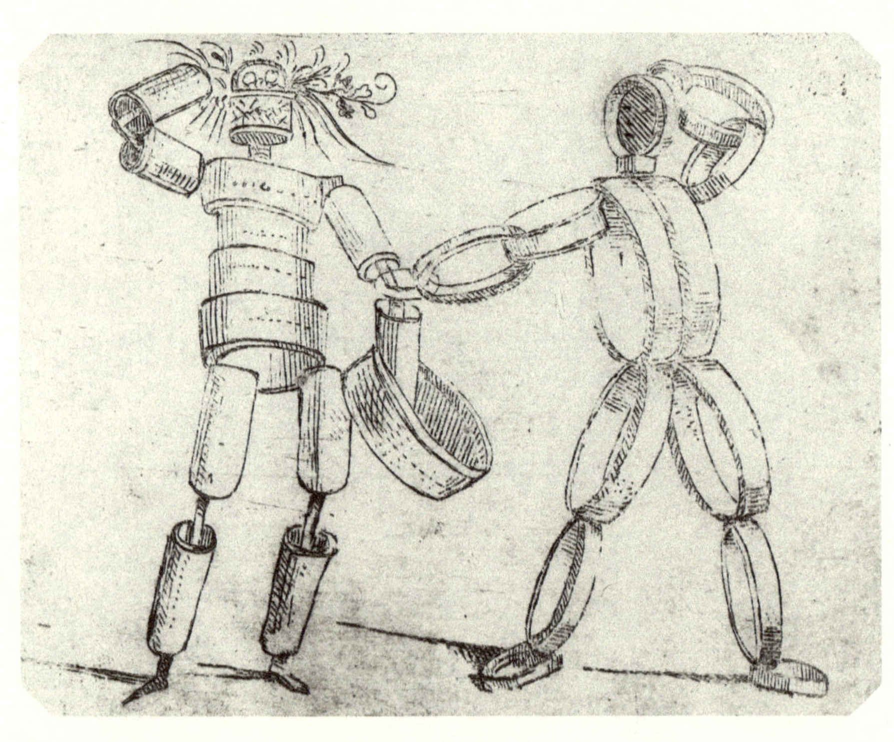

BETRAYAL

Even if you believe in words,
they act in bad faith
double-cross your best efforts
and desert you.

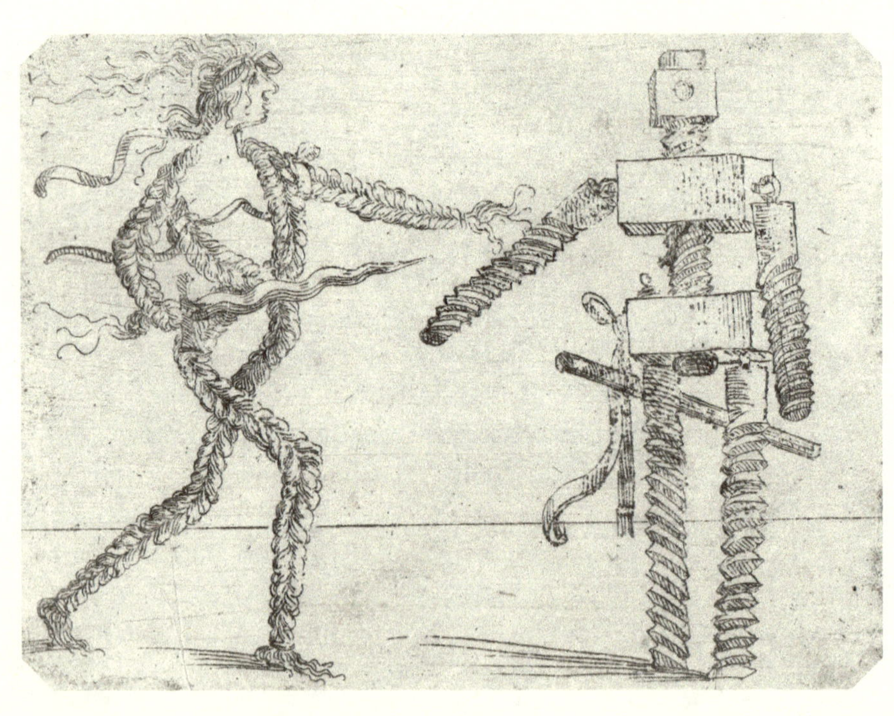

Backlit

The darkness I can conceive
goes beyond the benefit of words.
Hell shrinks that darkness to thinkable
but the unspeakable remains.

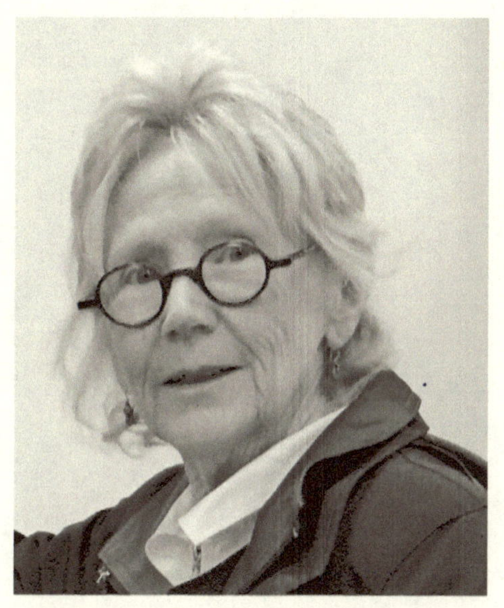

ABOUT THE AUTHOR

Bonnie Stanard writes short stories, novels, and poetry. Her work has appeared in journals such as the *American Journal of Poetry*, the *Wisconsin Review*, *Harpur Palate*, and *Broad River Review*, and her historical fiction novels and children's books are available at various online venues. Her poetry chapbook is currently available from Main Street Rag.

www.ingramcontent.com/pod-product-compliance
Lightning Source LLC
LaVergne TN
LVHW051013080826
845145LV00009B/2606